MW01100296

THE OFFICIAL
EXTREMEGOLF
MANUAL

For golfers with more attitude than aptitude

THE OFFICIAL

EXTREME GOLF

For golfers with more attitude than aptitude

Andrew Gellatly

Main photography
David Robinson

BARRON'S

First edition for the United States,
its territories and possessions,
and Canada published in 2005 by
Barron's Educational Series, Inc.
by arrangement with
The Ivy Press Limited

Copyright © THE IVY PRESS LIMITED, 2005

All rights reserved. No part of this book may
be reproduced in any form, by photostat,
microfilm, xerography, or any other means, or
incorporated into any information retrieval
system, electronic or mechanical, without the
written permission of the copyright owner.

All inquiries should be addressed to:
Barron's Educational Series, Inc.,
250 Wireless Boulevard
Hauppauge, New York 11788
www.barronseduc.com

ISBN-13: 978-0-764-1323-91
ISBN-10: 0-7641-3239-3

Library of Congress Catalog Card No.
2004116193

This book was conceived,
designed, and produced by
THE IVY PRESS LIMITED
The Old Candlemakers
West Street, Lewes
East Sussex, BN7 2NZ, U.K.

Creative Director **Peter Bridgewater**
Ivy Publisher **Sophie Collins**
Gift Publisher **Stephen Paul**
Editorial Director **Jason Hook**
Design Manager **Karl Shanahan**
Senior Project Editor **Caroline Earle**
Art Director **Wayne Blades**
Design **Balley Design Associates**
Illustrators **Wayne Blades, John Bradbury,
and Ivan Hissey**

Printed in China
9 8 7 6 5 4 3 2 1

CONTENTS

*fore*WORD

I've been accused by journalists of inspiring kids to hit real golf balls around town, terrifying their neighborhood. After this was cleared up, a close friend of mine commented, "as a kid, it's your God-given duty to break windows." I suppose that's what grabs us most about extreme golf—the innate sense of childhood freedom that it offers.

Traditional golf is seen by many as a stuffy game for dull and dogmatic people. Taking the fundamentals of golf and removing issues of class, race, finance, location, privilege, and tradition, leaves the inherent viewpoint of these kids. Whether any of the adaptations outlined in *The Official Extreme Golf Manual* are social commentary or carry a statement of anti-establishment, they all reiterate one thing—the beautifully simple concept of using a stick to propel a ball to a target and beat your fellow players. The many different manifestations of the game that this book addresses bring fashion and flamboyance back into traditional golf, all of which seem to have been frozen out over the past century.

Recently, Tiger Woods was attributed with the quote: "Golf is a sport for white men dressed like black pimps," and Hunter S. Thompson wrote his last article, "Shotgun Golf," in which golf and clay pigeon shooting meet head on. While these comment beautifully on the social position of golf, all participants in the events and activities in this book are proactive commentators on golf in their own right.

Next time you see someone with a set of clubs over their shoulder, walking downtown, taking the subway, or even in the supermarket, don't deny the most logical thoughts of all, including telling them that it landed behind the cheese counter. Then smile, like I do when my opponent is in a bunker.

Jeremy Feakes, Organizer of the Shoreditch Urban Open

introDUCTION

All a golfer needs is a target somewhere on the horizon, a club, and a ball. The rest is details and fences on the prairie. And, strangely, the harder it is the more we like it.

But lately the ideal of golf has been obscured by rivers of money flowing into the sport—money that has brought with it titanium drivers, a technology-fueled frenzy, primped and rolled billiard-table greens, and course fees that run to hundreds of dollars. Golf on TV is a high-stakes poker game played by tanned and increasingly joyless millionaires.

It was not always this way—golf was brought to life on the links courses of Scotland, on the marram grass and sand scrub between farmland and the sea. Bored shepherds took to knocking balls into rabbit holes. The Scottish coast is still a place where golf is life and nothing interrupts it, not the North Sea winds nor the grazing sheep, but you would be hard-pressed to remember that rough-and-ready spirit on the verdant fairways of Augusta.

This book, however, is about golf that takes place anywhere but on a golf course. It may be on the ice floe in Greenland or the frozen Bering Sea in Alaska. It may be in the Mongolian desert with a jeep serving as a makeshift golf cart. Increasingly it may be about playing in the fabric of the city in which you live—the cranes and wharves of Hamburg docks, the sidewalks of New York, or the tree-lined avenues of Buenos Aires.

A much talked-about youth explosion in golf has certainly brought kids to the sport. Tiger Woods is their poster boy, but the new golfers don't fit easily into the old clubhouses and attitudes that go with them. Every U.S. suburb and British town has one of these old-fashioned clubs with features such as "don't-park-here" signs, an antediluvian dress code, the captain must play through, children and minorities unwelcome, and so on. In the U.K. just 4 percent of golf club members are non-white. And it's hardly surprising that in the United States for every three young golfers that come to the game, two leave.

For a generation raised to extreme snowboarding or skateboarding around concrete parking structures, a country club with flowerbeds might be too tame anyway. The sort of golf it wants is, increasingly, not the same as its parents play. Why sign up for a crazily early 6:00 A.M. tee time when there are opportunities to play for free somewhere else? Indeed, in Scotland, the home of golf, only 5 of the 12 percent of the population who claim to play regularly are full-fledged members of a golfing establishment.

Extreme golf is the solution to an all-too-familiar problem. When asked what they would most like to do if they had more time, most people's answer worldwide is always the same—spend more time with their friends. With extreme golf that doesn't have to involve driving miles and paying vast membership fees. And if your friends are duffers, so much the better; urban courses give rise to

Play It Where It Lies > The "play it where it lies" rule applies in extreme golf as anywhere else, but in this extreme situation you may find you need a couple of hundred yards of rope, a harness, and a carabiner. Jim Griggs says, "We take the rules seriously in Wyoming and when it says 'play it where it lies' we do just that! At the end of a hard week of leading the photo workshop at the "University of the Wilderness" we always break out the "Black Jack" [Daniels] and have a go at the golf ball with the clubs. After passing the bottle around several times we convince the only real climber in the group to pose for us dangling off the cliff with a three wood and an old yellow ball jammed into the cracks in the rock face."

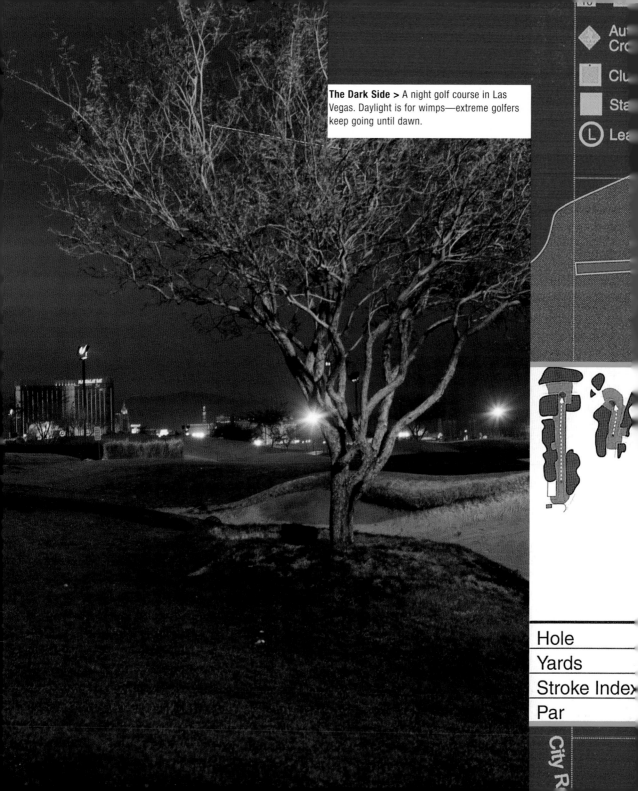

The Dark Side > A night golf course in Las Vegas. Daylight is for wimps—extreme golfers keep going until dawn.

Hole
Yards
Stroke Index
Par

City R

even more entertaining hazards. Balls roll under cars or into drains, and ricochet off telephone poles. Why play on an artificial irrigated and rolled course when the streets where you live are already full of opportunities for golf?

One indicator of an imminent golf boom in the cities came with Spike Jonze's seminal music video for Dinosaur Jr.'s "Feel The Pain." In the video a pair of Jonze's sharply dressed friends inhabit a semi-trailer truck for a clubhouse, and set off in their cart around Manhattan for a chaotic round of metropolitan golf.

Golf's propensity to turn perfectly rational people into gibbering, frustrated wrecks might make it a strange game of choice for the coolest of the metropolitan cool. Even more strange is the adoption of golf by hip hop artists—hip hop producers are, after all, ice cool. But a shared love of fashion and unusual partnerships are key to making it all work smoothly. Jeremy Feakes, founder of the Shoreditch Urban Open says, "It's all about putting a good player with a duffer, a dandy with a slob, or a humorous person with a dull one. My favorite pairing is Rodney P, the rapper, with Ronan Rafferty, the Ryder Cup player."

Paul North	Tabernacle	Leonard West	Paul Central	Clere	Paul South	Dysart	Holywell			Clifton	Scrutton	New North	St Lukes	Marks	Havey
2	3	4	5	6	7	8	9	**Out**	Initials	10	11	12	13	14	15
42	96	75	50	70	175	136	71	**835**		115	94	115	134	112	56
6	17	2	1	15	9	13	7			16	14	11	10	4	12
3	4	4	3	4	5	5	3								3

Bar Hopping > A scorecard from London's Shoreditch Urban Open— where the conflicting demands of par and bar meet.

RULES, *THREADS,* AND *STICKS*

Get in the swing with the new kids on the green

Knowing the rules, dressing right, and carrying the right equipment is halfway to success in most sports but for extreme golfers the rules are mostly about self-preservation, the dress code is permissive, and the equipment is as bizarre as you can make it.

RULES
NONE

75

Urban Threads

In theory, golf still represents white male elitism, a quintessential rich man's sport with collared shirts, cashmere Argyle sweaters, and polished spikes—but the day-to-day reality is rather less exclusive. Pleated, dot-com-era chinos abound, and pastel golf shirts and baseball caps that look like giveaways from a software convention have become all too normal.

On the professional tour only the Swedes Fredrik Jacobsen and Jesper Parnevik, and British Ryder Cup player Ian Poulter, dress with anything like verve, while Tiger Woods' wardrobe keeps a predictable number of dreary mass-produced garments flowing from the stores. Gone are the days of Payne Stewart's sadly missed plus fours and tam-o'-shanter —not to mention his habit of wearing the N.F.L. team colors of whichever club he was playing nearest. Bill Murray's outfits on the Pro Am circuit are still a reminder of the glory days of *Caddyshack*.

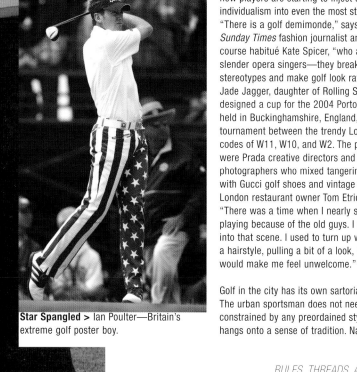

Star Spangled > Ian Poulter—Britain's extreme golf poster boy.

But away from the world-class tournaments, new players are starting to inject some individualism into even the most staid courses. "There is a golf demimonde," says British *Sunday Times* fashion journalist and golf course habitué Kate Spicer, "who are like slender opera singers—they break the stereotypes and make golf look rather sexy." Jade Jagger, daughter of Rolling Stone Mick, designed a cup for the 2004 Portobello Open held in Buckinghamshire, England, a golf tournament between the trendy London zip codes of W11, W10, and W2. The players were Prada creative directors and fashion photographers who mixed tangerine Pringles with Gucci golf shoes and vintage denim. London restaurant owner Tom Etridge says, "There was a time when I nearly stopped playing because of the old guys. I never fitted into that scene. I used to turn up with a bit of a hairstyle, pulling a bit of a look, and they would make me feel unwelcome."

Golf in the city has its own sartorial spin. The urban sportsman does not need to be constrained by any preordained style, yet still hangs onto a sense of tradition. Nat Turner,

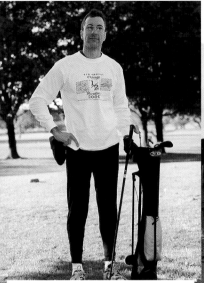

From Dusk 'Til Dawn > From mosh pit to sand pit—an N.B.G. regular extends a hard night's partying into a morning of golfing.

Dépêche Mode > Chicago speed golfer Jim Kosciolek trades spikes for running shoes.

Junkyard Chic > You may be playing in the local scrapyard but that doesn't mean you can recycle an outfit.

a dreadlocked white boy from Ladbroke Grove in London who plays at public courses in well-to-do Richmond says, "There's something nice about all the wood paneling and the tradition, about going about your business in a proper way. There is something to hold onto with the Englishness. I like the little lion on a Pringle sweater, you know?"

Vintage golf clothing is absolutely acceptable on the urban golf scene, as are garish pairings of Argyle, plaid, and leather. Though Hamburg's Natural Born Golfers (N.B.G.) have been known to play nude, they usually make an effort to include at least one item of N.B.G. brand clothing, often a belt buckle. For cold weather they have a subtle down-filled camouflage jacket, but most days a leather jacket and jeans will do. Lizard-skin cowboy boots are also advised, and the Hamburg crew are already collaborating with designers on a complete range of N.B.G. clothing.

The fashionistas of San Francisco's Urban Golf Association coordinate a wide range of thrift-store chic, but with extra cachet attached to

loud checks and bloated baggy plus fours. A whole new market is springing up to cater for the tastes of postmodern golfers.

A new generation of golfers who have only ever known the Tiger Woods era grew up on punk and thrash metal, but that doesn't make them immune to the pleasures of golf clothing; it just makes them very, very selective.

The golf clothing of the Rat Pack, J.F.K., and mobsters such as Sam Giancana is making a comeback too, but rinsed through a frothy wash of generational perspective. Brands such as Penguin and Arnold Palmer are popping up again. Italian-American lawyer Randy Riccardo has just resurrected the ailing DiFini golfing brand first made famous during the Eisenhower era. "I think it needed a whole generational jump for that stuff to come back," he says. "When you are sufficiently distanced from a time you can begin to cherry-pick the best of it. We can see what our parents could not see. They looked great; they were the apotheosis of ice-cold, scotch-on-the-rocks cool."

A wave of cultural celebrations of this Rat Pack cool—the movie *Swingers* and the remake of Sinatra's *Ocean's Eleven*, together with the return of martini bars and hotel-suite chic—has fed a desire to slip into a pair of flat-fronted fuchsia slacks or a russet silk roll neck. You can pair these fashion accessories with a mullet. Bad haircuts, mullet wigs, and so on do not in any way prejudice the game, and you have the look of a new era.

Now that fairways are interchangeable with runways, and fashion photographers can easily be found teeing up a new look at the same time as a new swing, purists may feel a twinge of concern. But while a connection with the roots of the game may be distant, it is never entirely lost from sight. During his experience of golfing across the Mongolian steppes, Andre Tolmé came across first-hand confirmation that Mongolia is the sartorial birthplace of golf. Archaeologists recently uncovered human remains in Central Asia that were covered in tartan plaid fabric. "Do we really need more evidence than this?" asks Tolmé.

Ice Golf Outfits

In golf you are often weathering one sort of storm or another, but if you can stay warm and look cool while doing it you'll feel so much better. Once you take your golf out of the city and onto the ice floe, then weathering the storm takes on a whole new aspect. Ice golf needs special snow gear—insulated Gore-Tex® boots, crampons (inch-long snow spikes), and UV-proof goggles are mandatory because the conditions on the course can drop from 41°F (5°C) to -4°F (−20°C) and from clear to white-out in a matter of minutes. Usually, six layers of clothing are recommended, beginning with silk underwear and topped with a couple of layers of fleece. You may also need a high-velocity rifle in case polar bears wander onto the fairway.

According to British journalist Dominic Bliss, who played in the 2004 Drambuie Ice Golf Championship in Svalbard, when it comes to ice golf clothing, layering is vital. "I was wearing about six layers on average, starting with a silk undershirt and moving up to a windproof breatheable jacket. It all has to be breatheable though, because as you walk around the holes and swing at balls, you do warm up a bit and any sweat will freeze."

Crampons are also essential because the biggest risk is falling over while taking a shot. "When you plant your feet to take a shot you really have to embed them in the ice," says Bliss, "otherwise you fall backward when you take your first swing." Add the necessity of steel clubs—graphite shafts shatter in the cold—and warmed bags for any camera or radio equipment and the weight of cart luggage grows exponentially.

Polar Technique > When the fairway turns into 6-inch (15-cm) deep ice crud, you need to dig your heels in for a firm footing.

Extreme Rules

The rules of golf apply equally to the game, regardless of whether it is played on rough or fancy courses. However, extreme golfers may have a few additions or variations of their own. Run-of-the-mill golfers will recognize many of urban golf's rules, but the most obvious ones are to be safe and have fun. "We tend to avoid big areas of plate glass," says Jeremy Feakes, organizer of London's Shoreditch Urban Open, "particularly on the dogleg holes." There are eight extra rules for the Shoreditch Urban Open but only two are routinely applied:

● You are entitled to take a free shot if your backswing could endanger a window nearby.

● A ball landing or rolling under a car necessitates a free drop one club's length away from the car.

PASTURE RULES

Rule number one of pasture golf is not to cut fences. However, when you enter or exit through gates, close and secure them behind you. PastureGolf.com—the on-line bible of pasture golf etiquette—suggests: "Go ahead and visualize Miss Manners out on the links if that helps make the point, or better yet, picture what happens when El Toro discovers that the gate is down and decides to take a stroll."

According to Charles Price, a writer for *Esquire* magazine, the entire handbook for pasture golf can be reduced to three rules:

1 Do not touch your ball from the time you tee it up to the moment you pick it out of the hole.
2 Don't bend over when you are in the rough.
3 When you are in the woods, keep clapping your hands.

Watch the Birdie > Quartzsite in the Arizona Desert is a winter nesting ground for flocks of snowbirds, but they need to dodge the occasional projectile.

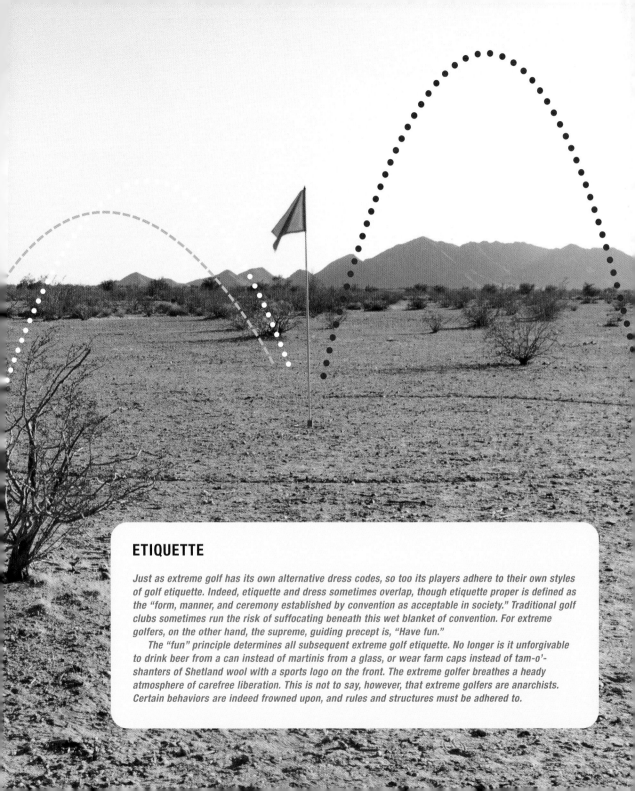

ETIQUETTE

Just as extreme golf has its own alternative dress codes, so too its players adhere to their own styles of golf etiquette. Indeed, etiquette and dress sometimes overlap, though etiquette proper is defined as the "form, manner, and ceremony established by convention as acceptable in society." Traditional golf clubs sometimes run the risk of suffocating beneath this wet blanket of convention. For extreme golfers, on the other hand, the supreme, guiding precept is, "Have fun."

The "fun" principle determines all subsequent extreme golf etiquette. No longer is it unforgivable to drink beer from a can instead of martinis from a glass, or wear farm caps instead of tam-o'-shanters of Shetland wool with a sports logo on the front. The extreme golfer breathes a heady atmosphere of carefree liberation. This is not to say, however, that extreme golfers are anarchists. Certain behaviors are indeed frowned upon, and rules and structures must be adhered to.

PASTURE GOLF

A selection of pasture golf course rules:

What Fore, Nixon, Texas
● You can golf and drink, golf and shoot, but not drink and shoot.
● Shooting your opponent's ball out of the air equals a hole-in-one on your next hole, but still counts as a stroke for him.
● Don't use your hands to retrieve your ball from the gopher holes on the fifth hole.

Smedberg Pines Golf Course, Pollock Pines, California
● Bear droppings count as "loose impediments."
● Don't spend more than five minutes looking for any one ball.
● Beware of cars on holes 4 and 12.
● Read yardages on every hole; it's a short course.
● See nothing, feel nothing, and be the ball.

WaTaShi Pasture Golf Association Course, Crawfordville, Georgia
● Rule 7 is, "You can cheat but if you get caught, fess up! No argument."

Ernie Holzemer's Four Hole Pasture Golf Course, Amidon, North Dakota
● No Golf Carts Rule—It would cut playing time down to five minutes.
● Gopher Rule A—"If a gopher steals your ball, don't mess with the gopher."
● Gopher Rule B—"If a gopher steals your ball, it's legal to retrieve it from the gopher hole."
● Seven-Iron Rule—"Use your seven iron to kill rattlesnakes."

Pasture Golf Course, Lackey Farms, Thorndale, Texas
● Dog Rule A—If a dog or coyote picks up your ball, you SUBTRACT one stroke, but you must play it from wherever the dog drops the ball.
● Dog Rule B—Only one dog bonus per hole allowed. Multiple pickups don't count. The first time the ball falls out of the dog's mouth, that's where you play it from.

(Source: www.LackeyFarms.com)

ALASKAN RULES

The Raven Rule—Muskeg Meadows Golf Course, Wrangell, Alaska
● If a raven steals your ball, you may replace it with no penalty, if you have a witness to the theft.

The Critter Rule—Birch Ridge Golf Course, Soldotna, Alaska
● Please allow moose and other wild critters to play through!

The Bear Rule—Bear Valley Golf Course, Kodiak, Alaska
● Bears have the right to play through.

Relief from Moose Tracks—Mt. Fairweather Golf Course
● Take relief from moose tracks.

Free Drop—North Star Golf Club, Fairbanks, Alaska
● If a raven or fox steals your ball, take free drop at theft location.

[Source: The Great Alaska Golf Guide by Karleen Grummett (Silverfox Publishing, 2000).]

Balls

The availability of a good, drivable, yet car-wind-shield-safe golf ball would revolutionize urban golf more than any other invention, but currently tournament balls are somewhere between a footbag and a wiffle ball with wildly unpredictable behavior on the green.

Golf scientists have been working on the problem for several decades. Back in the 1980s Troy Puckett, Wilson's top ball designer, created the Cayman Ball with pimples instead of dimples—developed for short Caribbean courses. The Cayman plays like a conventional golf ball in every way except to travel approximately half the distance. German sports equipment manufacturer Adidas is believed to be close to delivering a breakthrough.

But there is, of course, a trade-off. The more your ball behaves like a regular golf ball when it hits the sidewalk, the more likely it is to keep on rolling into the gutter. Many urban golfers still prefer to rely on a floppy lofted ball that comes to rest when it lands.

White Out > Fluorescent balls still allow spin and slice to be applied but what happens to the ball when it hits a sheet of smooth ice is another matter.

Clubs

The average length of an average player's drive has increased more than 20 percent in the past 20 years—a tribute to boron and graphite, and titanium, and ball technology. Tiger can hit 300 yards (274 m) with a three iron. It all adds up to long, busy fairways, early tee times, and more expense.

Realistically an extreme golfer is better off with ancient clubs from his dad's garage than fresh, individually tweaked, titanium-shafted beauties. A bag of irons from the local yard sale is ideal. Woods don't get much use in the extreme golf world—often the balls are in a bad state and that will destroy a wood fairly quickly. Concrete, rocks, and sidewalk gratings can even put nicks in your irons all too easily.

Speed golfers have developed a game that all but eliminates splurging on new clubs. Bob Babbitt, a speed golf pioneer, carries just an eight iron and a putter when he plays. Others carry just one club. "Some people use a small golf bag and carry their clubs in that because then they can keep their grips dry. But, honestly I've never tried that," says Babbitt.

No Excess Baggage > Speed golfers travel light when on the run—lightweight club bags and a minimum of four to six clubs.

Pimp My Cart!

In the Arctic, where there are no golf carts, ice golfers have to make do with snowmobiles, but for extreme golf on more solid surfaces the limited range of a typical battery-powered electric cart will likely prove too restrictive. While the Yamaha Golf-Car Company manufactures a new and powerful G-MAX four-stroke, many urban golfers still prefer the old-school, two-stroke gasoline-engined carts.

Harley Davidson manufactured a unique range of golf carts from 1963 to 1982 that are still sought after by fans of extreme golf. The tiller steering limits their stability at speed but in good conditions they can reach up to 30 mph (50 km/h).

There is a unique pleasure to be had in taking a down-at-heel, neglected cart and turning it into something cheery. Torsten Schilling, founder of Hamburg's extreme golf club, Natural Born Golfers, bought his first Harley cart on eBay for $5,000. It happened to be offered for sale by a neighbor of

Torsten's friend in North Dakota. Realizing that it was as expensive to ship one cart in a crate as four carts in a shipping container, Schilling then went about accumulating more carts from the American Midwest.

Indiana proved especially fruitful. The four N.B.G. carts are now safely back in Hamburg and one of them has already been granted a road license by the German ministry responsible for automobile registration. It is the first-ever licensed road cart in Germany, registered as a Harley Davidson mini-truck with a weight of 1,320 pounds

(600 kg). German car licensing requirements call for all occupants to have seat belts and to wear glasses or goggles.

"We get pulled over by the police about four times a day driving this," says Schilling, "but we just produce this piece of paper and they let us go."

In the inaugural Shoreditch Urban Open golf trolleys were immediately put to use as champagne coolers, while the clubs were carried by hand, but founder Jeremy Feakes is looking around for the right carts to use for subsequent events.

"Our idea of cart customization is quite subtle," says Feakes. "We don't want the carts to become the show. We want to leave the players to be the show, but we might, say, give them really long, whippy aerials."

Hart to Hart Cart > The 1970s Mercedes coupe cart—gorgeous like Jennifer herself.

Kraftwerk > N.B.G.'s Road-legal Harley Cart—too slow for the autobahn but perfect for *Strasse* golf.

" Our idea of cart customization is quite subtle. "

URBANGOLF

Golf in a civilized environment

From San Francisco's Washington Square Park to the docksides in Hamburg a new generation of metropolitan golfers are taking their nine irons out into the street and discovering the joys of the concrete fairway.

METRO GOLF

Under the Tarmac Fairway

Golf is never far away in the city. If you take a cab in London and the driver has to open the trunk to fit in your suitcase, chances are there will be a set of clubs in there somewhere, too.

On quiet afternoons London cab drivers sneak off to their favorite municipal courses, and play golf in that semicasual garb of slacks and polo shirt that characterize a working cab driver, but increasingly they are enjoying the chance to play in the streets where they pick up fares. London's Shoreditch Urban Open has brought Sunday golf to some of the busiest streets in central London. In San Francisco, the Urban Golf Association has pioneered bar-hopping golf with extreme outfits. Now other cities such as Berlin, Cape Town, and Seoul are getting the idea.

Ryder Cup competitor Ronan Rafferty's enthusiasm for urban golf—that grew when he played in the first Shoreditch Urban Open in 2004—is infectious: "There are people who are walking past who see us playing in the street in all this gear and they just get caught up in the atmosphere and become fans. I can anticipate a time where every supermarket and every school has a team—everyone can do it—not everyone can get out onto a real golf course; they don't have the time or money or for whatever reason, but everyone can get out and do this."

Cruise Control > The four-tier range at Chelsea Piers on Manhattan's Hudson River.

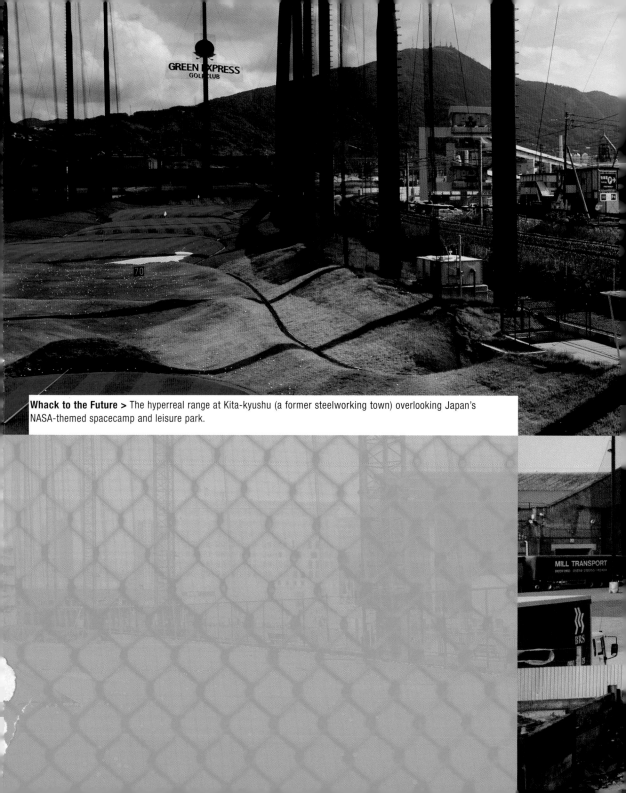

Whack to the Future > The hyperreal range at Kita-kyushu (a former steelworking town) overlooking Japan's NASA-themed spacecamp and leisure park.

GREEN EXPRESS
GOLF CLUB

70

MILL TRANSPORT
BEDFORD 01234-218055 782604

BRS

ome on the Range

range has a special place in the hearts and minds of golfers. Hunter S. Thompson's
ever published column was a musing, with Bill Murray, on the possibilities of shotgun
a new sport that would combine the golf driving range with the shooting range in a
level facility. European and American golfers are tiring of the high prices and sniffy
ce dished up by the mainstream golf courses; they are just following the example of
hese golfers, who long ago gave up on writing five- and six-figure checks to cover
al membership fees, and started to embrace the culture of the urban range.

untry such as Japan where the
r of golf fans far exceeds the acreage
ses available to play on, the driving
has filled a vital place in the lives of
s' salarymen" golfers, but without
omising standards, Japan's ranges
uch more than the bare bones of such
l whack. They have been able to add
he features of a normal golf course,

including showers, steamrooms, and bars, into a rooftop site. And
when Japanese range golfers practice the balls are delivered
mechanically, resting on a tee ready for hitting

In a truly innovative and groundbreaking departure Japanese
extreme golfers have already mooted a safari style tournament in
which teams will drive from range to range, sampling the hospitality
of each sport.

e to Range (outer pages) > On a
journey by bullet train from Tokyo to
saki the physical manifestations of
's growing golf obsession become
ent, with ranges occupying ever more
ne sites, making a range-to-range
feasible.

Après Shift > The industrial dumping ground behind King's Cross station in London proves popular with drivers of black cabs desperate to de-stress.

London—
Shoreditch Open

"What we do is very like golf," says Jeremy Feakes, president of the Shoredltch Golf Club and organizer of one of the U.K.'s fastest-growing golf tournaments, the Shoreditch Urban Open. "It has eight extra rules, but I just can't remember them at the moment."

The inaugural 2004 Urban Open saw 62 players chipping balls around an 18-hole course along the closed-off streets of Shoreditch, a bar and restaurant district in the East End of London, on a public holiday weekend in May. "This is London's playground anyway," says Feakes looking wistfully down Tabernacle Street, a pub-filled side road that in May is transformed into one of the first holes of the Urban Open. The proximity of pubs is vital to the success of the Shoreditch event, and "drinking is inherent in our golf," says Feakes. "There's an inherent humor in everything on the course and the drinking adds to that. I enjoy it and I drink all the way around."

Old brick warehouses still line the course but often they are topped with expensive penthouses where the new urbanites recline in self-parodic *Wallpaper* magazine absurdity. "All these rich people— they usually go home to the country on the weekend to see Mummy," says Feakes, "so we're just playing in their front yard while they're away."

Feakes and his friends took several years planning the first event, and they were able to get sponsorship from Ladbrokes, a leading U.K bookmaker, that enabled them to lay on astroturf greens and score-boards. "The details are what make people laugh," says Feakes. "For the next event we are planning a set of speakers on every green playing birdsong, but not just ordinary birdsong—birdsong played on a poor-quality system, really amped up and distorted."

The logistics of closing roads and controlling traffic, and the problems of balls going over walls and fences means urban golf can take as long as a conventional game, even if the course is shorter, but the compensation comes with extra drinking time. "It took about seven-and-a-half hours to get everyone around last year," says Feakes. "Bearing that in mind, most people are pretty much hammered by the end."

One of the golfers, who played under the pseudonym Davis Duffer Jr. III, was on his way home after a steady round of drinking and, not wanting to waste the opportunity, stopped off in a nightclub on the Kings Road. "My caddy and I ended up in a club in Chelsea till three in the morning, checking my clubs in the cloakroom and dancing on a podium still wearing my golf spikes," says Duffer Jr.

Lining up players for the Shoreditch Golf Club's tournaments is, predictably, a parody of the normal golf club application procedure. "Normally the best way to join a golf club is by being put forward and then seconded by someone," says Feakes. "In our applications we just ask people what their favorite bar is—we can pretty much tell by that. That or their favorite DJs."

Urban Golf Bag > Something we found lying around in the rough.

The Sidewalk Strut > Closing in on the curbside green on Dysart Street—the 8th hole.

The Shoreditch Golf Club is already planning foreign tournaments, most notably in Cape Town, South Africa, to take place on Freedom Day. "Freedom Day is all about celebrating the democratic vote, celebrating the right to make a statement," says Feakes, "but Cape Town is also synonymous with exclusive whites-only golf courses so we're looking to sucker some of those snobs. It's all about understanding the friction and making it play."

Wall-to-Wall Golf > The cream of London's graffiti artists have embraced golf's aesthetic potential.

RONAN RAFFERTY INTERVIEW

Irish golfer Ronan Rafferty, who won the European Order of Merit, has played in the Ryder Cup and the U.S. Open. He now commentates on golf for Sky TV, and was a willing participant in the 2004 Shoreditch Urban Open. "In normal golf sometimes you get the fortunate bounce off of a tree or a spectator," says Rafferty, "but I've discovered that in urban golf you are always looking for that."

Rafferty was filmed by a TV crew chucking his ball out of a basement parking garage after he failed to loft a shot clear as he attempted to take a shortcut across Paul Street—a moment of indignity that added to the glee of his fellow competitors.

"When you can get a ball that you can hit a hundred yards or more, that will transform the game," says Rafferty. "When I started last year I made the mistake of trying to whack the ball as hard as I could, but the real technique turned out to be just to hit it and run it along the ground."

But even some out-of-bounds balls and a little fence hopping has not diminished Rafferty's enthusiasm for the urban game: "I've played at the Masters and in the U.S. Open and the Ryder Cup, and in the finest golf courses of the Emirates, but this was up there with them. I'll probably never get to play golf on the moon but this was just as wacky. You're on the green and 20 feet away there might be a huge rotary. It's very strange to putt out right next to a rotary and a dual carriageway. The holes could be anywhere and you could make anything happen. I'd love to be invited back."

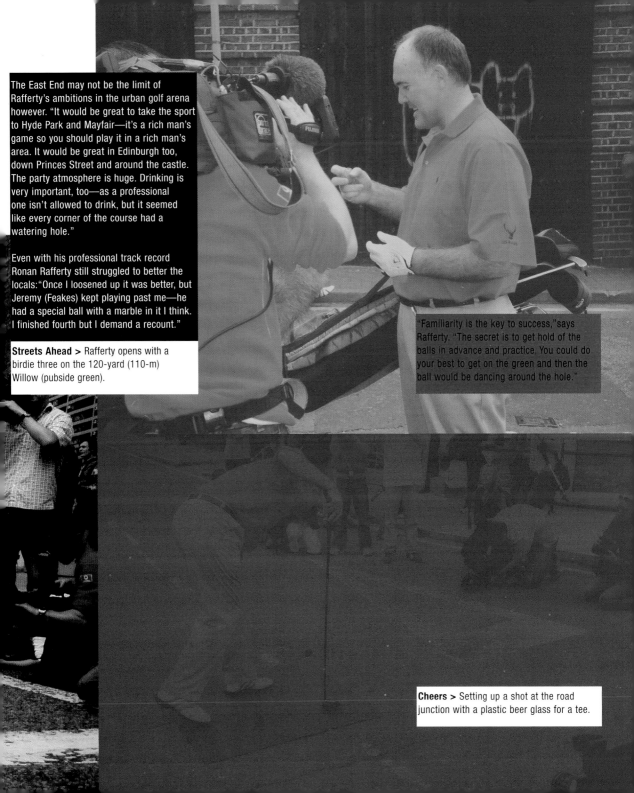

The East End may not be the limit of Rafferty's ambitions in the urban golf arena however. "It would be great to take the sport to Hyde Park and Mayfair—it's a rich man's game so you should play it in a rich man's area. It would be great in Edinburgh too, down Princes Street and around the castle. The party atmosphere is huge. Drinking is very important, too—as a professional one isn't allowed to drink, but it seemed like every corner of the course had a watering hole."

Even with his professional track record Ronan Rafferty still struggled to better the locals: "Once I loosened up it was better, but Jeremy (Feakes) kept playing past me—he had a special ball with a marble in it I think. I finished fourth but I demand a recount."

Streets Ahead > Rafferty opens with a birdie three on the 120-yard (110-m) Willow (pubside green).

"Familiarity is the key to success," says Rafferty. "The secret is to get hold of the balls in advance and practice. You could do your best to get on the green and then the ball would be dancing around the hole."

Cheers > Setting up a shot at the road junction with a plastic beer glass for a tee.

Hamburg Natural Born Golfers

At the end of a row of cranes on a wharf in Hamburg docks, a group of seven urban golfers are gathering for a Sunday morning round. But this version of urban golf goes beyond San Francisco or London's tournament games where there is an 18-hole course and a par for each hole. This is destruction—testing the limits of golf with holes and hazards drawn up on the fly. Tees can be on boats or the tops of skyscrapers; targets will be barges, dumpsters, or garbage cans.

"Sometimes the holes can be 1.2 miles (2 km) long," says Torsten Schilling, the charismatic founder of Hamburg's urban golf scene. "And they take up to two hours to play."

The first practice shot out into the Elbe River ricochets off a nearby crane's steel hawser and clatters onto the cargo-shed roof above us. Others fly past tourist boats out for a view of the harbor. Then they start to play for real on 500 yards (457 m) of railroad track and grass that run alongside the cranes.

The sheer volume of balls fired out into the Elbe River is breathtaking. Schilling reports one driving contest when they sent 2,000 range balls to the bottom.

Schilling, originator of the cult group Natural Born Golfers (N.B.G.) calls his urban events "cross golf"—golf in and around the docks. This isn't exactly tournament golf because improvised targets include containers, oil barrels, the buckets of excavators, wrecked cars, or barges floating in the river. And each hole is match play—it doesn't matter how many strokes you take so long as you get there in fewer strokes than your opponent. There is no membership fee, no dress code, no green fees, and no handicaps. In fact, the absence of handicaps is a determined protest against the stuffiness of German courses that, perversely, refuse to take new players unless they have an established handicap.

We make our way to the multistory parking garage to hit some balls around the roof, but the entrance to the roof is locked. This being Hamburg docks, with no shortage of places to fire off balls, we

reroute to the recycling yard where the doors are always open. We take turns driving balls from the weighbridge toward the inflatable Santa Claus that hangs from a crane about 80 yards (73 m) away.

N.B.G. has been the victim of its own popularity, but it is also fair to say that its televised stunts have always been attention-seeking in the extreme. From building a mock living room complete with couch, lamp, and television on a barge, and using it as a floating tee, to putting across the marble floors of Berlin's Reichstag, the group's media profile has been high.

Muddy Waters > An N.B.G. favorite—the extended bunker along the banks of the Elbe.

Extensive coverage in the German press brought dozens of Porsche-driving hipsters down to the docks to find N.B.G. members on Sundays and get a little vicarious urban golfing. Nowadays, however, meetings tend to be a little more low-key, with a typical gathering consisting of a small group of invited friends, accompanied by the group's pet mascot, a dog named "Turbo Hund." Even so, N.B.G.'s popularity has brought a 150,000-strong list of subscribers to its newsletter. In any city in the world, Natural Born Golfers can count on handfuls of passionate followers ready to show them the urban infrastructure—from Warsaw to Kuala Lumpur.

In summer 2004, an N.B.G. national tour took place in Leipzig, Cologne, Berlin, Duisburg, Frankfurt, and Munich. Berlin was the scene of the tour's only accident. About 3:00 A.M. at a radio station in the former East Berlin, two of the N.B.G. girls were fooling around in one of the Harley Davidson carts and crashed into a café table with ten or so golf fans sitting around it. "There were bodies flying everywhere," said Schilling. "One of the guys bruised his back pretty badly—he was black and blue from head to toe."

Natural Born Golfers has become so well known that its founder and sometimes as many as four assistants are employed half the year to organize the sponsored tournaments. Volkswagen's leasing division bankrolled their German tour and Microsoft has also waded in. "This is a perfect customer relationship-building tool," says Dirk Pinkvos, the head of

Junkyard Challenge > A midshot cigarette eases the crushing pressure of a tough dockside pitch hole.

the Volkswagen division who signed up for N.B.G.'s unique brand of inspirational golfing anarchy. Pinkvos took VW customers to the roof of the Intercontinental Hotel in Berlin where they drove balls into space toward a rooftop 150 feet (50 m) away.

N.B.G. has acquired enough momentum to be a full-time career for Torsten Schilling. "This is my passion and my lifestyle," he says. "I do what I love and it's the best job I've ever had. In every city in the world we have people to contact and we can play golf with them."

Full Steam Ahead > N.B.G. founder Torsten Schilling hits off down the tracks—N.B.G.'s signature skull and cross clubs logo on his jacket.

This is my
passion and
my lifestyle. ”

Urban Golf San Francisco
—CHARLES BUKOWSKI NORTH BEACH INVITATIONAL

In the five years since it began, San Francisco's Bukowski Invitational, and its sister tournament, the Emperor Norton North Beach Open, both organized by the Urban Golf League, have become two of the best-known urban-golf tournaments in the United States. But since the balls used are lawsuit-proof foam and the preferred clubs are putters, it is famous more for its leading-edge fashion and cocktail drinking than its elegant looping golf shots.

Rick Abruzzo, one of the Urban Golf Association's founders, describes its golf championships as, "Nine holes, nine bars, and not a nine iron in sight." According to Abruzzo, "The idea for a San Francisco Urban Golf League was hatched at a bar called Spec's in North Beach. Seemed like a bad idea then; it still is. But now we do two games a year, a northern and southern route, both starting at Washington Square Park."

A strong sense of style and fashion is critical to the whole experience and a San Francisco urban golfer is, as Rick Abruzzo notes, "Characterized by an incredible taste in plaid. The bad outfits give some kind of surreal legitimacy to the game." He says, "If we didn't have the golf outfits, I think folks would be a bit less tolerant of our activities."

The ethnically diverse streets of San Francisco's North Beach neighborhood provide the backdrop for the Bukowski Invitational and the Emperor Norton: "I think putting through Portsmouth Square, gently tapping your way through throngs of Chinese folks playing GO, is a real treat," says Abruzzo.

San Francisco's scene has shied away from sponsorship and mainstream media coverage: "Drink specials from the bars is as close as we get," says Rick Abruzzo. "We don't want to make a commercial event out of this. The $5 fee covers the materials cost and a big BBQ for everyone who helps me out. But there is a company named AlmostGolf in LA that makes 'urban' golf balls and sponsors our events."

In Search of the Miraculous > Rick Abruzzo relies on divine intervention.

BADGE OF HONOR

My personal favorite moment was in the first year. The southern route has a hole in front of a small Franciscan church. The game was on Sunday and the priest was deeply upset that we were playing golf as his congregation was leaving. We talked him down and he blessed our clubs. Later at 5:30 when we're all done and drunk, one of the golfers found a bag of T-shirts in an alleyway that said: "America welcomes Pope John Paul II—1987." God loves Urban Golf. I still wear mine with pride.

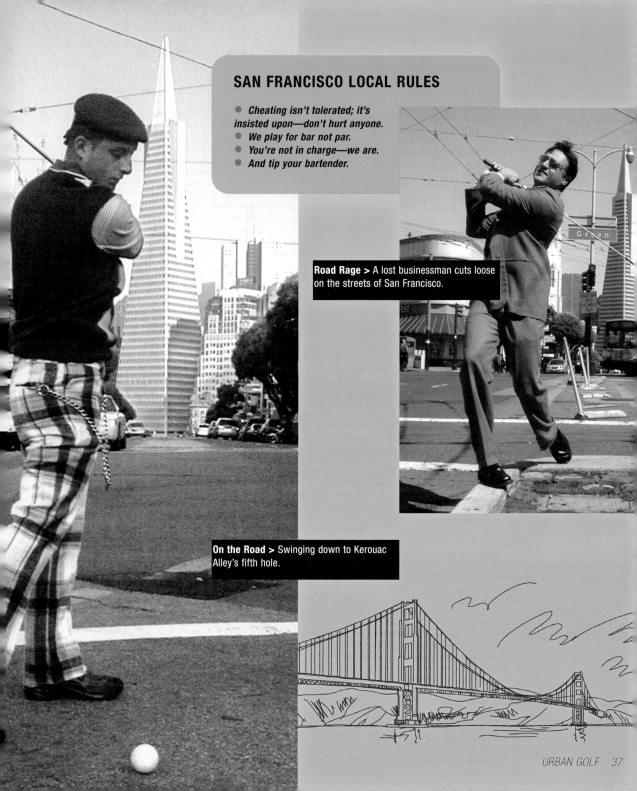

SAN FRANCISCO LOCAL RULES

- *Cheating isn't tolerated; it's insisted upon—don't hurt anyone.*
- *We play for bar not par.*
- *You're not in charge—we are.*
- *And tip your bartender.*

Road Rage > A lost businessman cuts loose on the streets of San Francisco.

On the Road > Swinging down to Kerouac Alley's fifth hole.

Urban Golf in New York

New York City was quick to adopt the urban golf phenomenon—indoor ranges and courses opened in sheds in Chelsea back in the 1980s. These sheds have since become contemporary art spaces and Manhattan real estate prices have forced golf out of the chain-link cages, indoor crazy-golf sheds, and driving ranges, and onto the streets. By 2004, golfers could be found in Times Square doing their thing to publicize a new console game called Outlaw Golf.

New York State is not the most golf-friendly place in America—in Albany, the city council has a by-law forbidding the playing of golf on the streets, but Manhattan and the other boroughs, as so often happens, have led the way with a liberal approach to street golf.

Even if golfing is technically prohibited in Central Park, an early indicator of an imminent golf boom in Manhattan came with Spike Jonze's seminal 1994 music video for Dinosaur Jr.'s song, "Feel The Pain."

In the video, which Tiger Woods subsequently referred to in one of his Nike ads, a pair of Jonze's nattily dressed friends inhabit a semi-trailer truck for a clubhouse, and set off in their cart around the streets of Manhattan for a chaotic round of metropolitan golf. Their round takes them through Central Park, Columbus Circle, and to a green on top of the Pan Am building.

Other boroughs have been quick to pick up on the sartorial and entertainment potential of the sport. Brooklyn urban golfers particularly warm to the sound of leather golf balls against cars and storefronts.

Manhattan Golf Boom > By 2004, extreme golf had spread to Times Square (see also pages 40–41).

ROOFTOP LAYUPS

Anyone can lay up from a manicured fairway, but try doing it from the roof of a mini-block, across six lanes of traffic, and into a target zone that's no bigger than the trash can outside the front door of Barnes & Noble! Since backspin is not an option, only awesome accuracy will keep you in play and still in the game.

TEEING OFF

With the Flatiron Building looking majestically over you, the tee position
is guaranteed to generate an adrenaline rush. The Tiger line takes you
to the roof of the Urban Outfitters Building on Broadway, alongside
the Flatiron. The less ambitious can try a controlled fade down the
sidewalk when a gap in the crowds permits.

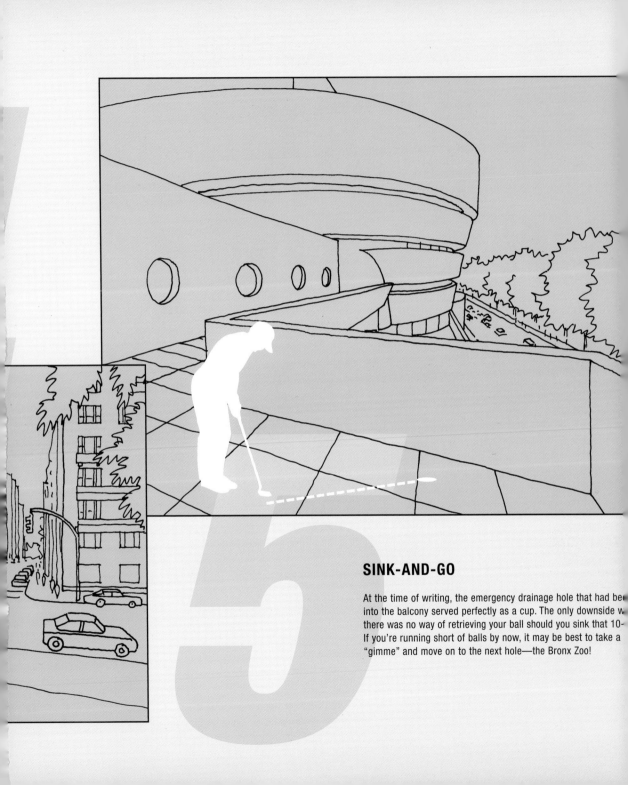

SINK-AND-GO

At the time of writing, the emergency drainage hole that had bee
into the balcony served perfectly as a cup. The only downside w
there was no way of retrieving your ball should you sink that 10-
If you're running short of balls by now, it may be best to take a
"gimme" and move on to the next hole—the Bronx Zoo!

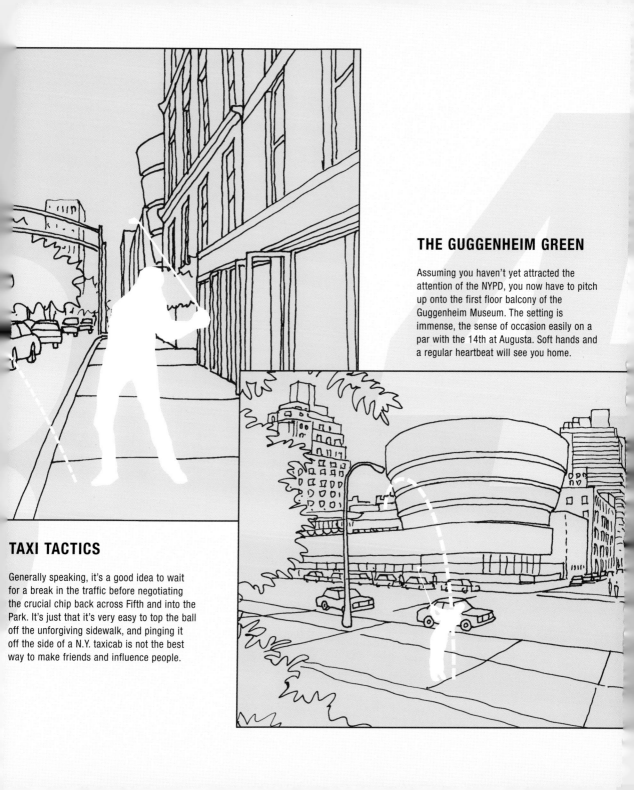

THE GUGGENHEIM GREEN

Assuming you haven't yet attracted the attention of the NYPD, you now have to pitch up onto the first floor balcony of the Guggenheim Museum. The setting is immense, the sense of occasion easily on a par with the 14th at Augusta. Soft hands and a regular heartbeat will see you home.

TAXI TACTICS

Generally speaking, it's a good idea to wait for a break in the traffic before negotiating the crucial chip back across Fifth and into the Park. It's just that it's very easy to top the ball off the unforgiving sidewalk, and pinging it off the side of a N.Y. taxicab is not the best way to make friends and influence people.

CROSS*GOLF*

Golfing out of bounds

As an alternative to mountain biking, bungee jumping, or white-water rafting, golf has traditionally been a long way behind in the adrenaline stakes, but with the right approach extreme golf can make prime cuts for extreme sports channels on TV.

GOLF
ROCKS

Safety First > Cross golfers have been known to mutate in the chemical waste of the Highlands.

Bogged Down > Slogging through the boggy moorlands of northern Scotland.

Missing Links

Scotland, with its golfing heritage and its endless miles of featureless heather, has found itself at the forefront of cross- or mountain-golf development.

Hikers with no previous interest in golf have found themselves inexplicably drawn to whacking brightly colored balls. The Missing Links Challenge organized by Ayrshire golfer Mark Sim has already chalked up a number of single-target mountain challenges in the hills and mountains of Scotland, including an attempt on the 2,300-foot (701-m) Tinto Hill in Lanarkshire, a journey across the Isle of Arran, and a trip through the Galloway Forest.

The U.X. Open®

The U.X. Open's founder and managing member is Rick Ryan, an experienced sports marketer who developed the event by combining his enthusiasm for golf and skiing with the rocketing popularity of adventure sports. U.X. golf caters to beginners as well as veterans, and hiking skills may prove as useful as putting technique.

The inaugural U.X. Open was staged on August 27, 1999 at Mountain Creek Resort in Vernon, NJ, but by 2004 the tour had grown with four qualifying events (at Mammoth Mountain, Bromley, Wildcat, and Snowmass) with the championship final at Snowmass.

The U.X. Open has ten simplified rules catering to the rocky terrain. They include: a four-club limit; instead of putting, participants must pitch the ball onto a painted circle 20–30 feet (6–9 m) in diameter; less severe than normal penalties for lost balls and unplayable lies; and no dress code—although hiking boots are strongly recommended. Yardage markers and golf carts are redundant in these conditions— laser rangefinder binoculars and ski lifts are preferred.

The 2004 U.X. Open was dominated by California golf pro Ric Moore, on his third trip to the U.X. Open Championship. After finishing third in 2002 and as the runner-up in the following year to his former high school and college golf teammate Ed Galvan, Moore reached the top of the mountain in 2004. He defeated Galvan in a sudden death chip-off, to earn the right to wear the U.X. Open winner's red velvet jacket with zebra stripes.

U.X. OPEN CHAMPIONS

- *1999 Kevin Cahill of Berwyn, PA, at Mountain Creek (Vernon, NJ)*
- *2000 Jim Ryan of Rochester, NY, at Snowshoe Mountain (Snowshoe, WV)*
- *2001 Peter "Mongo" Schory of Chewelah, WA, at Holiday Valley (Ellicottville, NY)*
- *2002 Peter "Mongo" Schory of Chewelah, WA, at 49° North (Chewelah, WA)*
- *2003 Ed Galvan of Burbank, CA, at Snowmass (Snowmass Village, CO)*
- *2004 Ric Moore of Bakersfield, CA, at Snowmass (Snowmass Village, CO)*

The Pillar Mountain Golf Classic

Back in 1984, in a Kodiak bar, Glenn "The Cod Father" Yngve posted a "C Note" on the bar challenging fellow fisherman Steve "Scrimshaw" Mathieu to beat his score in a golfing contest to the top of nearby Pillar Mountain.

Right then the Pillar Mountain Golf Classic was born—a par 70 one-hole tournament. With sponsorship from the Professional Cross-Country Golf Association it now attracts golfers from all over the world to challenge the local talent. The course elevation gain is 1,400 feet (427 m). Having a spotter in the deep snow of late March is helpful, but use of two-way radios, dogs, and chainsaws is prohibited. Hatchets and hand tools are permitted. Also, cutting down power poles is prohibited, and cursing tournament officials carries a $25 fine.

Northern Exposure > If you choose to accept this challenge bring tools and a noisemaker to warn local bears of your presence.

Elfego Baca

Every June a handful of extreme golfers tee off from a wooden box clinging to the side of a New Mexico mountain and the only way is down a near-vertical cactus-covered fairway.

In the annual Elfego Baca Shoot golfers play one hole down Socorro Mountain fighting diamondbacks and scorpions along the way. The tournament is limited to ten golfers who are driven in all-terrain vehicles to the 7,243-foot (2,209-m) mountain peak for an early-morning tee off. From the peak the par 50 hole winds down the mountain to a distant pin (a 50-foot/15-m diameter clearing known as "The Hole") 2½ miles (4 km) away and 3,000 feet (915 m) below the summit. Each competitor is allowed up to three, very necessary, ball spotters and is accompanied by a course official who is also the scorer. The final score is calculated on the number of strokes taken to reach the clearing, plus the number of lost balls. Mike Stanley has won the event 18 of the 19 times he has played it. "My tactics are to send the spotters down the mountain to where I think I might hit the ball," he says, "and then I try to hit them with the ball—which I have never managed to do."

The Road to Kalgoorlie > On Australia's longest, straightest highway you may need to disengage cruise control as you round the first bend for 300 miles (483 km).

Outback Golf—Australia's 850-mile links

Taking a truly extremist view of golf, some outback councils in the western Australian desert are planning to open the world's largest golf course along the Eyre Highway spanning the border of Western Australia and South Australia.

More structured than Andre Tolmé's Mongolian route (*see pages 46–49*), the Australian course will definitely need a driver—the holes are likely to be up to 70 miles (112 km) apart—but the unorthodox course with oiled sand greens will offer the chance to play some of the most remote, snake- and spider-infested desert in the world.

Councils along the length of the Nullarbor Plain, a treeless desert that crosses three time zones, have now approved construction of the course. They hope it will induce tourists to slow down and appreciate what is regarded as one of the most desolate environments in Australia. There will be one hole at each of 18 towns and roadhouses (gas stations with cafés) stretched along the Nullarbor section of the

Eyre Highway from Kalgoorlie, 450 miles (724 km) east of Perth, to Ceduna, 500 miles (804 km) west of Adelaide. Collectively, the holes will be known as Nullarbor Links.

"It's not going to be St. Andrews by any stretch of the imagination," says Alf Caputo of the Kalgoorlie-Boulder tourist association, "But it's going to be something unique to this region." With parts of the highway passing close to the ocean, at the Head of Bight, for example, golfers will also be able to enjoy some whale watching from the cliffs there.

The first seven holes are in South Australia, between Ceduna and the western Australian border. Motorists will stop at a roadhouse, play a hole, and then drive to the next hole—62 miles (100 km) down the road in some cases.

The idea for the course comes from Balladonia's roadhouse manager and frustrated golfer Bob Bongiorno, who is looking to boost tourism and find new friends to go golfing with.

"I brought my golf clubs when I first came out here seven years ago and tried hitting a few balls in the bush," he said. "I had to fight the spiders to get them back, so I've not used them in ages." Bongiorno says about 300 vehicles pass along the golf course section of Eyre Highway each day, a distance that, if driven at the speed limit, takes 13 hours to navigate. Mr. Bongiorno's own roadhouse in Balladonia will provide one of the biggest attractions of all. It is built next to the site where the U.S. Skylab space station came crashing to Earth in 1979, and the prospect of golfing around craters left by lumps of crashed space junk should excite all but the most jaded highway golfer. "Even if people play only a few holes, it will break up their journey and give them the chance to say they've played on the world's biggest golf course," he said.

The roadhouse manager also plans to build the world's largest golf ball in Balladonia to publicize the course. Dimensions are to be finalized. Trial holes will be built in stages—the first at Balladonia—and the course is scheduled to open in 2006.

Walkabout > If you see Uluru (Ayers rock) you know you're lost.

Mongolian Golf

On July 10, 2004 Andre Tolmé set a new level in extreme golfing when he became the first person to golf across Mongolia. The steppes of Mongolia, once the home of Genghis Khan and the ferocious Golden Horde, have now been opened up to extreme golfers. Thanks to Tolmé's Internet Weblog, extreme golf fans all over the world were able to follow his epic hit fest that, though divided into 18 designated holes, actually covered a distance of 1,320 miles (2,124 km).

Tolmé teed off in Choybalsan, an old Soviet Army garrison town in Mongolia's far east, facing the Chinese border, on May 28, 2004. He then covered the total fairway distance to the city of Khovd in a par-establishing 11,880 strokes over a period of seven weeks. Taking each major town to be a golf hole, Tolmé established a route that skirted the world's largest bunker, the Gobi Desert.

Tolmé drew the line at golfing through crowded markets and busy streets. He would pocket the ball upon arrival at a settlement, walk through the town and then tee up again on the other side. "You hit the ball," he said, explaining his technique for playing on a land without fences. "Then you go and find it. Then you hit it again. And again. And again." On one occasion he found a poisonous snake curled around the ball, protecting it as if it were an egg.

For overall navigation the Mongolian golfer found his way from hole to hole using a G.P.S. receiver and a compass. I use the tee only when I start a hole," said Tolmé, adding that he plays by "winter rules because Mongolia can often be cold."

Tolmé walked the first three holes, carrying all his equipment on his back, but taking the knapsack on and off led to exhaustion problems. He explained how the weight begins to take its toll on an extreme golfer: "I tend to hit poor golf shots, which means more lifting of the pack, more exhaustion, more poor golf shots, spiraling downward."

While his problems were partially solved when a local craftsman made Mr. Tolmé a small cart for his equipment (he carried just a three iron and a four iron for the trip), he came to rely completely on his caddy, a former soldier named Khatanbaatar, who carried water, food, and a tent in a Russian jeep that was fitted with a fetching customized upholstery of hand-woven rugs.

Tolmé, whose handicap is 15, decided on his 2,322,000-yard (2,122,308-m) round of golf after a visit to Mongolia two years before when he decided it was the world's most naturally formed golf course. The open rolling countryside and the presence of at least 30 million grazing animals in the country to mow the fairways is also a big bonus, making the landscape ideal for a low-key distance game.

There are also obvious difficulties with Mongolian golf, however, not least the ferocious wind that tears across the steppes. *Salikh*, the Mongolian word for wind, is the golfer's worst enemy. A typical steppe breeze blows at a brisk 15 miles (24 km) per hour but on windy days that speed can triple. On the first hole a storm nearly blew away Tolmé's tent as he was sleeping inside. "I yelled to Khatanbaatar to stand on the tent as I gathered what I could to shove into the jeep," said Tolmé. "When I opened the tent flap, things began to fly off like bullets into the darkness. Outside was a maelstrom of blowing sand. We stood only a few feet apart but had to yell at each other to be heard above the wind and blasting sand. It would be conservative to say that this wind was gusting at 80 mph (130 km/h) with the sand biting into our eyes and faces as we labored to make it to the jeep."

Tolmé, a civil engineer from New Hampshire, was lucky enough to be able to treat this enormous Central Asian nation as his private course and he found the Mongolians who fed him mutton, mutton fat, and sheep's milk along the way to be completely supportive of his adventure. He was often invited into yurts to drink hot milky tea, or sometimes vodka. In particularly inclement weather, when rain and lightning bolts lashed the steppes outside, this hospitality would extend into prolonged drinking sessions culminating with everyone falling asleep inside the yurt. While this drinking did nothing for his game it helped relieve Tolmé's pain caused by blisters, sunburn, and neck ache.

The Final Green > Tolmé overcame snakes, bugs, and rodents to secure his place in Mongolian golf's, admittedly small, hall of fame.

"When I say I am American, the universal response is, 'Ah, America, very good country, we like Americans,'" says Tolmé. Many Mongolians are followers of Tibetan Buddhism, and their outward-looking friendliness also comes from a suspicion of Communist China and its colonial ambitions. Tolmé's 18th hole passed by the wall of Chinggis (Genghis) Khan. As Tolmé observes: "It's not much of a wall anymore, nor was it built by Chinggis Khan (he was expanding his empire, not walling himself in), but it is still a reminder of the great history that this country possesses. The Mongolian Empire of the 13th and 14th centuries still remains the largest empire that the world has ever known."

After 1,200 miles (1,931 km) of golfing Tolmé came to see the final approach to the city of Khovd as his golfing grail: "This is my 18th green at Augusta," he said. "I know I'll never be a good enough golfer to add my name to the list of those who have triumphed at the Masters—Nicklaus, Palmer, Woods. But I know another thing. The list of those who have golfed across Mongolia is a very short list. As of now, there is only one name." Nonetheless there are now signs that Mongolians are awakening to their golf potential. Last year in Ulan Bator the first golf course opened, complete with horse-mounted caddies who charge after balls, marking their locations with flags on arrows. Moreover, the first indoor driving range has opened, also in the capital,

"You hit the ball, then you go and find it."

which was Tolmé's sixth hole. Some commentators argue that Mongolia could in fact leapfrog the country club phase of golfing, and embark directly on cross golfing and find a national golfing identity hitting balls through unorthodox settings such as city parks and streets.

IMPORTANT FACTS AND FIGURES

- *Mongolia is about three times the size of France.*
- *Mongolia has a human population of 2.6 million but is home to more than 30 million livestock.*
- *Forty percent of Mongolia's population is nomadic.*
- *The average altitude in Mongolia is 5,184 feet (1,580 m); the highest point is 144,337 feet (4,370 m) above sea level.*
- *With 100 percent of property occupied by its owners, Mongolia has the world's highest percentage of private housing.*
- *Taiwan officially considers Mongolia to be part of its territory.*
- *The gerbil originated in Mongolia.*

Don't Fence Me In > Mongolia's friendly locals and rolling hills make the country an ideal candidate for the title of the world's largest golf course but the cross-winds can be punishing.

*PASTURE*GOLF

The game au naturel

It may add value to your home to be next to a Arnold Palmer-designed 18-hole course but would you really want to join any club that would have you as a member? Across the nation golfers are opting out and playing across fields and pasture, fences, and prairies.

DIRT
GREENS

Putting in the dirt

It may seem perverse to hack a golf ball around fields where farm animals graze. Yet the prairie and pasture golfers among us—and this may be a little hard for the manicured-turf specialists out there to swallow—prefer it that way.

The advantages of prairie golf are huge. First, the courses call for hardly any of the pesticides, fungicides, and watering of ordinary courses. Plus, with pasture golf, farmers get more use out of agricultural land, still get tax breaks and don't have to move the animals. Moreover, you can play without waiting in line for green fees as little as $1, though $3 is about usual. Maybe it doesn't yet amount to a full-blown backlash, but while the $24 billion U.S. golf-course industry rolls ever more devilish, fertilizer-sucking acreage, with greens on islands or whimsical bunkers the shape of toes, a small but determined group of golf fans want to play on what they have, and metropolitan golfers are chomping at the bit to sample some of this genuine country-style ambience instead of cookie-cutter sameness.

The grounds on which golf is played are called links, being the barren sandy soil from which the sea has retired in recent geological times. In their natural state links are covered with long, rank, bent grass and gorse. Links are too barren for cultivation but sheep, rabbits, geese, and professionals pick up a precarious livelihood on them.

Sir Walter Simpson

Willie Nelson owned a golf course in Texas that some believe he lost to the government when he was sued over income taxes. Asked what par was on any given hole, Willie said, "Whatever I make it." On tour the legendary country singer would often have his tour bus stop in the middle of nowhere for a meditative early morning session of whacking golf balls into the brush.

As the Pasture Golf Aficionado Society explains: "To make fairways like carpets and greens like pool-table tops may eliminate bad lies and bounces, but it also eliminates a true part of the game. We suspect that most golfers who complain about weeds in the fairway don't like to play golf in the wind."

The spread of pasture courses is widening because the land doesn't need to be given over solely to golfing. Bear Valley Meadows Golf Course in Seneca, Oregon, has a helicopter landing pad between the first and second holes. In Wisconsin the Argue-ment Golf Course of New Glarus is a 2,260-yard (2,065-m), par-36 ex-dairy farm.

The Road to Hell

The Nevada and Arizona Deserts are better known for their UFO activity than their golf courses but fans of pasture golf have taken to spraying their lakebeds with vegetable dyes and marking out unirrigated greens on some of the most desolate expanses of white clay in the world.

Take a two-hour drive north from Reno and pay the $50 entry fee and you can participate in the Annual Black Rock Desert Classic. Doug Keister, a professional golf photographer, founded the Black Rock Desert Classic in the late 1980s. The original event has grown in scale from a three-hole birthday party bash for his friends to a full-on, nine-hole 3,900-yard (3565-m) course that attracts more than 50 players at a time.

The Black Rock Classic is marked out in the middle of 300 square miles (777 sq. km) of playa-desert floor that is so cracked and pitted that local rules allow you to tee up the ball for every shot. None of the greens is green and the holes that Keister has given names, such as the Vortex and the Freeway, are more like dislocated living rooms or crime scenes transported to the desert. One has a body-shaped chalk line next to a standard lamp, a TV, and a couch.

The midday heat brings temperatures up to a balmy 90°F (32.2°C) in the winter, but, with no water in sight, a heat haze adds a surreal quality as golfers tee off toward coffee tables and TVs on the baked horizon.

The best-known hole is called Hell, a 700-yard (640-m) moonscape with a deeply fissured green that has been painted as a diabolical flaming ball. Keister is happy to emphasize the performative aspect of the event: "I wanted to give people an experience they can't get anywhere else," he says.

Beam Me Up > Quartzite, a nine-hole course that straddles the Central and Pacific time zones in Arizona, gives golfers a perfect excuse for an extra hour's play. Quartzite's golfing twilight zone is free to play but with an honesty box for those who want to contribute to its upkeep.

Christmas, Florida

Driving east on Highway 50 from Orlando to Cocoa Beach through Florida's strip malls and swamps, the itinerant golfer would be delighted to find the Christmas 9-hole backyard course with year-round reindeer.

This backyard course in a small town called Christmas says everything about the pleasures of pasture golf. No formalities—just drive in, park, and play after paying the recommended $5 green fee. You then have a choice of the owner's pair of golf carts nestling under the car port. This is the sort of course that requires touch and talent more than technology and new clubs, and best of all a foursome can get around in under an hour. The year-round Santas and reindeer decorating the course are just a bonus.

Where's Santa? > Reindeer guard the first hole.

Christmas Cheer > Golfing isn't just for the holidays.

Lackey Farms, Texas

"It's like playing tennis in the backyard with string for a net," says a regular.

Lackey Farms meets every definition of a pasture golf course including the most obvious one—it is actively involved in providing fodder for ruminants. As a rule, modern golf courses bear very little resemblance to their ancestral roots, however this one does. The use of fertilizers, pesticides, and herbicides is outlawed.

The Lackey Farms Pasture Golf Course in Thorndale, Texas, features horse-drawn buggies for golf carts. Don and Beth Lackey run the course while waiting for their vines to become established. They harvest hay between some of the holes and warn smokers to watch out for grass fires.

Lawn Moo-er > Traditional techniques can help reduce course maintence costs on the pasture golf course.

SPEED*GOLF*

Grip it...rip it...run like hell!

Like a golfing version of the Olympic Biathlon, speed golf rewards those who can keep their heart rate under control long enough to make a shot, but those who try it report a strange feeling of liberation.

QUICKIE
GOLF

Run for the Hills

Tired of five-hour rounds endlessly delayed by shuffling zombies? Speed golf may be the answer. Certainly it's the fastest-growing sector of U.S. golf right now.

Because it's played on a regular golf course, strictly speaking speed golf should be disqualified from this book. However, the spirit of the game truly does transform an ordinary golf course into something completely different—a racecourse.

Speed golf is an individual, 18-hole, low-score competition. Open division contestants are allotted 49 minutes to complete a round of golf. Women and seniors (50+ years) have 59 minutes. Additional minutes count as penalty stokes, and caddies (driving carts) are mandatory.

Played in the early morning with a bag containing running shoes and one or two clubs, a round will usually be over in an hour. "You don't see unhappy faces," says International Speed Golf Association founder Jay Larson, "because speed golfers don't have time to get upset." Golfers in a hurry have often been tempted to tear around anyway; Steve Scott, an American record holder in the one-mile (1.6 km) run, went around a course in 1979 in less than 30 minutes, shooting a 95 with just a three iron, but it doesn't count as true speed golf unless the time and score are taken together.

Speed golf as a discipline was founded in 1988 by P.G.A. professional John Bell. His version of speed golf added the golf score to the equation. Surprisingly, players often discovered that running between strokes made little or no impact on their scores, in fact, some played better, because many golfers spend too much time agonizing over each stroke, and the ticking clock takes away that problem.

Dick Coop, a sports psychologist at the University of North Carolina who has been the swing coach for several top players including Corey Pavin, Larry Mize, and Payne Stewart, explains it: "Think about the amount of time between actual shots in golf. If you look at a guy shooting free throws in basketball, the opposing coach can call a timeout on him and freeze him out. In football the other coach calls a timeout before the field goalkicker gets a chance to kick, to freeze him out. In golf, you have every chance to freeze yourself out before every shot. It's not a continuous-action game."

"I have to confess. I am not a good golfer," says Bob Babitt, the Arizona-based self-proclaimed speed-golf dude. "I will shoot between 100 and 110 if I play in one hour or seven days. Good golfers will find the same results. Fitness golf may sound like an oxymoron, but I swear there is no better feeling than going out when the sun is just coming up and running on a beautiful golf course."

Breaking Sweat > Tim Scott, placed second in the 2004 Chicago Speedgolf classic.

Fast and Furious

Speed golf, like surfing, is one of those sports that gets otherwise sane men and women out at dawn. "I'd do this all the time if I didn't have a full-time job," says Jim Koscioiek, organizer of the Chicago Speedgolf Classic.

As the promoter of one of the leading U.S. speed golf tournaments, Jim Kosciolek is a strong advocate for the sport he loves.

"We call it extreme golf but it's also known as speed golf—in another variation there's one-club golf. But ours is like regular golf played at speed at a really professional level. Generally, when people start playing speed golf they shoot 4 or 5 shots higher—but some people play better. You're not standing over the golf ball thinking how to do it—that's when you get nervous and tense. With this thing you just take a shot and get on."

"In Oregon we have speed golf at Bandon Dunes, which is a top 50 course. It's a bit too long and too hilly for speed golf but we do it there because the guy who owns it loves speed golf and gives it to us for free."

"It's not exactly like the biathlon where you need to control your heart rate. Unlike pulling a trigger, with speed golf shots you don't have to be perfectly still. In fact its more rhythmic than normal golf. Putting is maybe a little bit closer to the biathlon—there you have to calm yourself because it's a much shorter motion. But people struggle at putting anyway. . . ."

"Generally, as long as we're paying for it the courses will do it but not many people will just allow morning play and the players don't want to pay full price if they're off the course in an hour. Our fantasy would be for courses to let us all on for two hours every Wednesday morning, say."

"The most established players, like Tim Scott and Chris Smith have been playing for ten years. In some ways it's been really frustrating because it hasn't really taken off—it's too hard to get courses to cooperate. But Tim and Chris shoot par or under par in under 45 minutes. And speed golf hooks up two great demographic groups—runners and golfers. It's really appealing for guys that are just getting out of college. What's really interesting is to watch really good golfers and runners playing together. You can see someone hit a 310-yard drive, then run after it, take a nine iron, and get it onto the green and birdie in."

"It's much more fun than other forms of extreme golf because the guys who play this are really good, and they love it. It gives them a four-to-five mile run and a round of golf. I'd do this all the time if I didn't have a full-time job."

"We need to get someone to sponsor it because right now all we're really doing is keeping it alive with four or five tournaments each year. There are a couple in California and one in Minneapolis, which is run by guys from Chicago. If we do it it's usually chosen to be at the right time of year when it's colder."

"Speed golf helps your regular game. You think, 'if I can do that running then I should be able to play it standing still.' Plus you don't take a full set with you so you learn to play imaginative shots. It definitely really helps your regular game."

"In older versions there were carts. Now most people carry lightweight club bags and most people take four to six clubs: a putter, some kind of wedge, some kind of driver, and an iron in the middle. You set off every four minutes and play by yourself."

Short On Time > Christopher Smith sprints to a victory in the professional division of the 2004 Chicago Speedgolf Classic.

Speed Golf's History

As well as promoting the game, Jim Kosciolek is also something of an authority on speed golf's history.

"Steve Scott is usually credited with inventing speed golf but dozens of people got out there with one club before him. But really it's not that important; we started it and that's important and my guess is that lots of people have at some time or another played it. Right now there are no concrete plans for a circuit—the biggest obstacle to that happening is the need for a sponsor who can come up with purses to attract people. We think we might have some hope with companies that involve speed and precision, maybe courier companies like FedEx."

"It'll be a great deal for the first sponsor to pick up on it—it attracts an inordinate amount of attention—people really pick up on it when it comes to their course. We just want to get it off the ground."

"People get in touch from Iceland and Malaysia, so we're not sure how big the world speed golf scene is but we will work with anyone who wants to get a tournament going. If you can get it right for people who go to work at 9:00 A.M., then they can get to work out and play 18 holes before 9:00 A.M."

Rules on the Run

It's tough enough to keep track of your score when you're running, so some speed golfers score with a system where they just count up their birdies (2 points) and pars (1 point).

Otherwise, speed golf follows all of the Royal and Ancient rules but with the time-saving amendment that you don't have to take out the flag to putt, although you still have to rake your sand traps and repair your ball marks. "In tournaments," says Jim Kosciolek, "we do what people do normally, but we might skip a couple of rules if it's getting really serious."

ICE*GOLF*

Let it snow

Inhabitants of Arctic countries have rarely let snow and ice hold them back from enjoying their favorite sport—fluorescent balls have long been available, but only recently has ice golf attracted a frenzy of tournament-style activity.

BREAK THE ICE

Ice Ice Baby

Ice golf is like ordinary golf except it takes place in that Twilight Zone *episode where the world just keeps getting colder and colder. The players wear six layers of thermals and the greens are plagued with polar bears.*

By far the best-known ice golf event is the Spitsbergen Open Ice Golf Championship, formerly named the Drambuie World Ice Golf Championship because the Scottish liqueur manufacturers sponsored the event for its first four years. The tournament itself is a 36-hole competition played over two days. The day before the championship the players also compete in a Ryder Cup-style tournament. Because there are no golf carts in the Arctic, the players and cameramen televising the event have to make do with snowmobiles.

In just four years this tournament has grown from a media event to a serious competition. It began in Uummannaq, Greenland, and after a cancellation in 2003 due to bad weather conditions, the 2004 Drambuie World Ice Golf Championship moved its location to a stunning ice fjord near the town of Longyearbyen in the Svalbard Islands near Spitsbergen. Svalbard, with a population of just 3,000, sits halfway between Norway and the North Pole and is home to one of the most northerly settlements in the world.

"The main problems are the temperature and the unpredictable weather," says British journalist Dominic Bliss, who competed in the 2004 Championship. "One day it can be quite sunny, the next it will be a full whiteout."

The nine-hole course at Svalbard is split into two sections; the first few holes are ice on top of solid ground but then players move out onto the frozen fjord to play on sea ice that is 10 feet (3 m) thick. At the water's edge occasional tufts of grass disappear to be replaced by lumps of ice where waves have frozen.

"Sometimes a ball would land and skid on smooth ice for hundreds of yards," says Bliss. "Other times it would drop dead into a pile of snow. And finding a lost ball can take hours. The only time you were sure of any shot was on the greens, which were called the whites, where the snow was smoothed out."

While the locals occasionally use the course after it has finished its role as the tournament venue, the local wildlife is quick to reclaim the area, with reindeer chomping on any exposed grass.

Warming Up > Practice sessions are key for judging distance.

An unusual danger in Svalbard is that of polar bears; in particular, mothers with young cubs may attack anyone approaching their lairs. Because of this hazard the outlying holes have armed guards with rifles to shadow the golfers. Fortunately, so far no golfer has been injured when actually playing in the championships, but 2004 victor John Wells broke his arm by slipping on the ice on the way back from the prize giving.

The Kiss of Cold Steel > Arctic temperatures help ice golf champion John Wells keep his cool during the final shot.

SPITSBERGEN OPEN ICE GOLF CHAMPIONS

There have been just four winning title-holders, including female professional golfer Annika Östberg from Denmark, the only woman golfer who has taken up the ice golf challenge and who managed to beat all of her male competitors.

- *2004 John Wells, England*
- *2002 Roger Beames, Scotland*
- *2001 Annika Östberg, Denmark*
- *2000 Annika Östberg, Denmark*
- *1999 Peter Masters, England*

"Nome has no trees of its own; it's too far north."

On Ice / 8

Bering Sea Ice Golf Classic

Golf fans in Nome, Alaska, understand cabin fever. At the end of a long, gloomy winter they look forward to a round of golf to coincide with the world-famous 1,049-mile (1,688-km) Iditarod Trail Sled Dog Race. Hence the creation of the Bering Sea Ice Golf Classic, played on the shores of the frozen Bering Sea.

Few golf tournaments can rival the unusual challenges posed by playing on semi-frozen sea ice. The course crosses pressure ridges in the Bering Sea and a growling sound of shifting ice can be heard frequently. Nome has a sea wall built about 30 feet (9 m) high to protect the town from storms. Golfers tee off from this sea wall, and the ball drops down onto the frozen Bering Sea itself.

During the next five holes of this six-hole tournament, brandy-guzzling contestants whack orange balls off "tees" that are actually spent shotgun shells. The pins are coffee cans drilled into the ice.

Local golfer Lois Wertz says, "The challenge of this particular course is that there are spots where it is very slick and icy. Even a little touch with your putter will send the ball several hundred yards. Then there are other areas where it is slushy and the ball stops dead." In earlier years organizers loaded fire extinguishers with green Jell-O and sprayed "greens" onto the course, but this practice has now been rendered obsolete by the use of artificial turf. Players must use a caddie, "preferably a sled dog with a taste for Budweiser," according to one local.

Temperatures hover in the teens and low twenties Fahrenheit. Polar bears are only one hazard; an ice shift can also instantly produce a large body of water not anticipated at tee time.

Happily, one tradition has been preserved: the duffers must still dog-leg around dense stands of used Christmas trees frozen onto the "snowways." Classic coordinator Eliot Staples remarks, "Nome has no trees of its own; it's too far north. So holiday pines have to be trucked in. Once stripped of their Yule finery, the trees are planted in the ice, creating a seasonal national forest." The forest was dreamed up by Connie Madden, after a local man stuck his old Christmas tree in the middle of the ice to aggravate a neighbor. Connie instituted the large-scale Christmas tree forest that has its own fans among the local population. Unfortunately, exotic wildlife is also attracted out onto the ice to eat the trees, and it has included visitors such as a walrus, polar bears, a musk ox, a reindeer, and some penguins.

Players themselves come dressed up as polar bears, in chicken outfits, or in old-fashioned golf costumes, complete with Argyle socks, sweater vests, and tams. And that's before they stop at the Breakers Bar for some pregame antifreeze.

I'm Still Standing > While hungry bears and reindeer are frequently spotted on the course, the main risk is simply falling over—spiked boots help ice golfers get a grip.

Ice and Snow Golf Events

WINTER GOLF TURNIER
Engadin, Switzerland
The hills near St. Moritz are alive with red balls for a nine-hole course whose "clubhouse" is the Silvaplana Sport Center.

BEAVER PRIDE WINTER GOLF CLASSIC
Bemidji, Minnesota
In January, Lake Bemidji is transformed into a frozen version of a famous course.

POLAR ICE CAP GOLF TOURNAMENT
Grand Haven, Michigan
Part of Winterfest, the tournament plays on a course carved across Petty's Bayou.

SNOWSHOE GOLF TOURNAMENT
McCall, Idaho
On the McCall Golf Course, snowshoes are used for spikes and tennis balls for golf balls.

CHILLY OPEN
Wayzata, Minnesota
Staged on Lake Minnetonka, the event drew 1,245 participants last year. P.G.A. star and Wayzata native Tim Herron has taken part.

MICKEY DUDE FOUNDATION CASA WINTER GOLF-ON-SNOW OPEN
Lincoln, New Hampshire
Loon Mountain foursomes on skis, snowshoes, or snowboards take a chairlift to an 18-hole "course" cut into a trail.

HEMSEDAL WINTERGOLF
Hemsedal, Norway
The annual tournament attracts many of Norway's top skiers, including world champion Lasse Kjus.

ATTITASH BEAR PEAK ON-SNOW GOLF TOURNEY
Bartlett, New Hampshire
Players are encouraged to wear costumes and must play on skis or snowboard.

THE PILLAR MOUNTAIN GOLF CLASSIC
Kodiak, Alaska
What began as a barroom wager between two local fishermen has become an annual one-hole, par-70 event up to the top of 1,400-foot (427-m) Pillar Mountain.

ARVIDSJAUR WINTERGOLF
Arvidsjaur, Sweden
Reindeer caddies escort skiers around this course from February to April. Open until the thaw.

ICE-GOLF SAFARI
Pöykkölä Ice Golf Course, Rovaniemi, Finland
The Lapland Safaris package includes an entire day above the Arctic Circle.

Annual Arctic Open Golf Tournament, Lake Eli, Minnesota
Played every February on frozen Lake Eli, Clinton MN. It is the longest-running golf tournament on ice.

Idlewild Golf Course, Sturgeon Bay, Wisconsin
The home of the Frozen Foursome and the Tundra Golf Association.

Ice Pack > You may not be able to beat them, but you can join them at the numerous ice golf events around the world.

EXTREME *GOLF*
DANGERS

At least getting hurt means you can tell the story...

FDR, a president known for his love of golf, famously noted: "The only thing you have to fear is fear itself." But in the world of extreme golf the dangers can be more tangible.

NO PAIN
NO GAIN

Risky Business

Extreme golfers take risks that have more in common with those taken by big-game hunters or adventure travelers. One look inside an extreme golf first-aid kit should reveal insect repellent, sun block, snake-bite serum, antihistamines, and splints for broken bones.

As soon as a round of golf turns into a hike any combination of bruising, biting, and scratching is possible. Golf in Central Asia, or indeed any large land mass, has a number of rodential and reptilian dangers, not to mention ever-present insects.

Mongolian golf adventurer Andre Tolmé faced bubonic plague-carrying marmots, four types of poisonous snake, and swarms of flies and mosquitoes, but he quickly developed a Zen-like approach: "I just ignore them no matter how many are covering my face, head, back-pack, or golf club." Even American mountain courses such as Elfego Baca or the U.X. Open present dangers from black gnats and terrifying cactus plants.

Some risks are best faced head on however; ice golfers who run the risk of polar bear attacks are well advised to employ armed guards near their outlying fairways.

In war zones and former war zones extreme golfers face the ever-present danger of unexploded mines and munitions, and should take guidance from local peacekeepers or mine removal specialists.

In South Africa, even the best-prepared fairways can come under attack by hungry warthogs, and crocodiles emerging from the water hazards. Warthogs can be aggressive and shooing an irate warthog away can easily dismantle the focus of any golfer. The Lost City in Sun City, pictured opposite, is particularly famous for its pit full of Nile crocodiles.

MOON GOLF?

THE*FUTURE*

Houston we have a bogey

When Alan Shepard struck a six iron shot on the surface of the moon in 1971 he estimated that the ball traveled "miles and miles." No doubt about it then, low-gravity environments could be great for any extreme game. But even before interplanetary golf travel becomes mass-market, entrepreneurs here on Earth are making sure that golfers craving new sensations will never be disappointed.

Stimulating Simulators

The world of computer gaming has taken to extreme golf already. Outlaw Golf, a game created for Xbox, has already raised the stakes for traditional golf simulator games by adding features from the world of extreme golf. The playing characters include wannabe rappers and bikini-wearing babes, while a cart-driving feature allows the golfer to perform cart tricks such as donuts, jumps, and slides in a race to raise their composure meter. Low composure will cause the player to have trouble making good shots, while high composure will allow the player to make great shots with very little effort.

In addition to the game's five regular courses, golfers can play over the Arctic tundra of Glacier Ridge or into the steamy jungles of Aztec Acres, and the same system that allows a player to vent rage by performing golf cart tricks also lets you beat up your caddie to build calm and increase composure. Obviously these techniques may not win an extreme golfer any friends in real life but for the days when conditions are just unplayable, extreme golf simulation games may provide the solution.

Anyone who watched Bill Murray play down an emerald fairway toward Mt. Fuji in the movie *Lost in Translation* will realize that virtual indoor golf environments are getting better all the time, though they

too are becoming more extreme. With three-dimensional projection capabilities and the possibility to generate any hole in the world virtually in a decent-sized room, there is no reason why the indoor golfer should be limited to playing Valderrama, the Old Course at St. Andrews, or Pebble Beach. Fifth Avenue is equally possible, as is the Grand Canyon.

Beam Me Up > Shepard's three lunar iron shots earned him a place in extreme golf's pantheon.

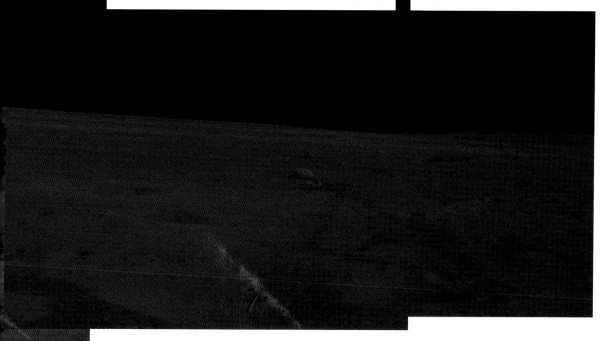

A Perfect World

How would you like a round of golf on the 50th floor of your apartment building overlooking San Francisco Bay or Puget Sound? Would the chance to putt out on a floating course in the middle of Lake Geneva appeal? These options may not be farfetched as architects learn to combine modern architecture with modern golf.

Golf courses feature regularly as seductive bait in real estate developers' brochures. In the Algarve in Portugal and in the suburbs of Las Vegas they are there to beckon would-be buyers in with a vision of recreation and nature. But the vision is hollow—like the make-believe idealized towns of Seaside and Celebration in Florida, they are all front. What 21st-century golfers crave is playing opportunities built into the fabric of urban life.

Harty & Harty, a London-based architecture firm, has visualized a sexy vertical golf course to be housed inside a spidery-framed glass high-rise. With the right toughened glass any residential or office tower can give over a few floors for an awe-inspiring three-dimensional golf course, with metropolitan golfers playing across architectural voids and chasms, and pulling carts across vertigo-inducing suspended causeways. The holes can be constructed across a sequence of floors adding height or depth as required, with bulging, udderlike supports separating the levels.

With a golf course inside your building you can play all night long without interruption and dark nights and thunderstorms will never present a problem, just an enhancement of the playing experience. Helicopters and birds pass at eye level.

Other architects have followed suit by designing offshore golf courses on floating mile-long city rafts.

Already, shrewd businesses in London and New York have started to incorporate the highest-tech urban ranges into their bars and restaurants. A company named Urban Golf Soho has opened a golfing facility in a bar in London's well-known entertainment district, where players can sip wine or drink beer, while progressing through any of dozens of courses.

Not everyone is ready to abandon the traditions of the conventional golf course—the hierarchy, dress codes, and membership fees, nor the unfortunate environmental consequences. People still have very different ideas of what constitutes a perfect golfing world. But extreme golf enthusiasts are working hard to create other utopias—real and imagined—that are thought-provoking enough to make even the most staid traditionalist stop and look.

Par in a Bar > More and more nightspots are catering to urban golf fans.

Where Eagles Fly > Harty & Harty's vertical golf course—coming soon to a high-rise near you.

DIRECTORY
Pasture Golf Courses

No need to book! Look for a piece of pasture in your neck of the woods:

Alabama
Indian Hills Golf Course
127 Par Private Drive, Decatur, Alabama 35603

Alaska
Fishhook Golf Course
Matanuska Valley near Palmer, Alaska 99645

Arizona
Bert Lee Park Golf Club, Arizona

California
Smedberg Pines Golf Course
Pollock Pines, CA

Colorado
Cow Chip Country Club
P.O. Box 770717, Steamboat Springs, CO 80477

Idaho
Swede Hill Golf Course
1445 River Road, Buhl, ID 83316

Iowa
Hi Point Golf Course
3533 Taft Avenue SE, Iowa City, IA 52240

Raleigh World Golf Course,
11859 550th Ave, Norwood, IA 50151

Kansas
Dinosaur Dunes Golf Club
1000 Pawnee Road, Shields, KS 67839

Lake of the Forest Golf Club
406 Lake Forest, Bonner Springs, KS 66012

Massachusetts
Country Club of Billerica
51 Baldwin Road, Billerica, MA 01821
Stowaway Golf Course
121 White Pond Road, Stow, MA 01775-1366

Missouri
Fayette Golf Club
Hwy 5 & 240, Fayette, MO 65248

Long Hollow Ridge Golf Course
Lincoln, MO

New York
Twin Pines Golf Course
Route 374, Cadyville, NY

The Meadows Golf Center
42565 State Highway 28, Margaretville, NY 12455

North Dakota
New England Golf Course
New England Golf Association, New England, ND 58647

Oklahoma
Gordon Golf Course
800 S.W. Gordon Road, Claremore, OK 74017

Oregon
Bear Valley Meadows Golf Course
12 Valley Way, Seneca, OR 97873

Doltonwood Golf and Country Club
15111 Springwater Road, Oregon City, OR

Pennsylvania
Pine Marsh Golf Course
Route 287, Oregon Hill, PA 16938

Texas
Lackey Farms Pasture Golf Course
801 County Road 439, Thorndale, TX 76577

Utah
Cherokee Springs Golf Resort
P.O Box 428, Hatch, UT 84735
www.cherokeespringsgolf.com

Virginia
Green Acres Golf Course
Newstead Lane, Cartersville, VA 23027

Washington
Sheridan Greens Golf Course
91 Sheridan Road Republic, Washington 99166
(Near Republic off Highway 20)

Wyoming
Salt Creek Country Club
P.O. Box 203, Highway 387, Midwest, WY 82643

Canada
Annie Lakes Golf Course
South Klondike Hwy, Whitehorse, Yukon Territory

Eighteen Pastures Golf Course
29110 Matheson Ave, Mission, BC V2V 6H5

Greenway's Greens
Box 42, Watson Lake, Yukon Y0A 1C0

International Pasture

Australia
Yanchep National Park Golf Course
(An Hour from Perth, Western Australia)

England
Golf Course Road, Painswick, Gloucestershire GL6 6TL
(Junction 11A off M5. Take A46 Bath Road toward Stroud. Entrance
on right, ½ mile before Painswick

New Zealand
Coromandel Golf Course
145 Woollams Road, Coromandel

Scotland
Bruntsfield Links
32 Barnton Ave, Edinburgh EH14 6JH

Melville Golf Club
Lasswade, Edinburgh EH18 1AN

Lochcarron Golf Club
Lochcarron, Strathcarron, Lochcarron IV54 8YU

Speed Golf

Silverbell Golf Course
3600 N. Silverbell, Arizona
Contact: John Bell, (520) 749 9655 x 627
www.azroadrunners.org

Extreme Golf Tournaments

Interested? Take on the best in their field:

SPEED GOLF

Awsome Eight Golf Challenge
Telephone: 44 20 8875 8890
www.awesomeeight.com

The Chicago Speed Golf Classic
www.speedgolfinternational.com

CROSS GOLF

Elfego Baca Shoot
Socorro Peak, Socorro, New Mexico
Telephone: 1 505 835 8211
www.hiltonopen.com

Pillar Mountain Classic
Alaska
Stop in at Tony's Bar (unofficial clubhouse) and ask.
Or you may write to Pillar Mountain Golf
P.O. Box 1906, Kodiak, AK 99615
Telephone (Tony's Bar): (907) 486 9489
http://chiniak.net/pillar/

The U.X. Open
UXGA Tour Properties, LLC 107 Post Road East
Westport, Connecticut 06880
Telephone: 1 203 255 2891
www.uxopen.com

ICE GOLF

25th Annual Arctic Open Golf Tournament: Big Stone Lake Wisconsin
127 Center Street
Clinton, MN 56225
(320) 839 3284
(800) 568 5722
Fax: (320) 839 2621

World Ice Golf Championship
P.O. Box 202, DK-3961 Uummannaq
Greenland
Telephone: 299 95 15 18
www.greenland-guide.gl/icegolf/

URBAN GOLF

Shoreditch Golf Club

The Shoreditch Urban Open
Shoreditch Golf Club, London
England

The Edinburgh Urban Open
Scotland

The Cape Town Urban Open
South Africa

www.sgcgolf.com/
Other International City tournaments by request

Extreme Links

Club Car
P.O. Box 204658
Augusta, GA 30917-4658
Telephone: (706) 863 3000

Cologne Cross Golfers, Cologne, Germany
www.crossgolf.com

Future Golf
http://www.fat.co.uk/fatgolf.html

Natural Born Golfers, Hamburg, Germany
www.naturalborngolfers.com

Sun Mountain SpeedGolf Carts
www.bogeybustergolf.com

The Tundra Golf Association—suppliers
http://www.octanecreative.com/tga/tundraads.html

Urban Golf—Virtual Range
London
www.urbangolf.co.uk/

Urban Balls

The AlmostGOLF company
1537 16th Street
Santa Monica, CA 90404
Toll-free: 800 998 1077
Fax: 310 496 1957
Info@almostgolfball.com
http://www.almostgolfball.com

The Cayman Golf Company
P.O. Box 5287
Albany, Georgia 31706
Telephone: 1 800 344 0220
info@caymangolf.com
http://www.caymangolf.com

INDEX

Acknowledgments

Picture Credits

The publisher would like to thank the following organizations and individuals for their kind permission to reproduce the photographs in this book. Every effort has been made to acknowledge the pictures, however we apologize if there are any unintentional omissions.

Jacob Brooks/Kodiak Daily Mirror: 44 top.
Corbis: 13 bottom right (John Gress), 55 (James L. Amos), 68–69 (Nik Wheeler).
Drambuie: 15 (all images), 19 top, 60–67 (all images).
Jim Griggs, Selective Focus Photography: 9.
Harty & Harty: 72 bottom.
Stacey Irvine: 36 bottom left.
NASA: 70, 71.
Andre Tolmé: 47, 49.
Mark Warmus: 36 and 37 center and right.
UXGA Tour Properties, LLC: 43 bottom right.
All other photographs by David Robinson.